The Aquinas Lecture, 1974

MAN AS
INFINITE SPIRIT

Under the auspices of the
Wisconsin-Alpha Chapter of Phi Sigma Tau

By

JAMES H. ROBB, Ph.D.

MARQUETTE UNIVERSITY PUBLICATIONS
MILWAUKEE
1974

Library of Congress Catalog Card Number 74-76084

Dedicated to the memory of my parents

Anna Eloise Robb
and
James Gilbert Robb,

and in gratitude to my sister,

Helen Kathleen Robinson

Prefatory

The Wisconsin Alpha Chapter of Phi Sigma Tau, the National Honor Society for Philosophy at Marquette University, each year invites a scholar to deliver a lecture in honor of St. Thomas Aquinas. This year is the 700th anniversary of St. Thomas' death, March 7, 1274. The lecture commemorating this anniversary was delivered on Sunday, March 10.

The 1974 Aquinas Lecture *Man as Infinite Spirit* was delivered in Todd Wehr Chemistry by Professor James H. Robb, professor of philosophy, Marquette University.

Professor Robb was born on April 25, 1918 at Bena, Minnesota. He earned the B.S. degree at St. Cloud State Teachers in 1940, the A.B. at Marquette University in 1948, the M.A. at Toronto University in 1950, the L.M.S. at the Pontifical Institute of Medieval Studies (Toronto) in 1952, and the Ph.D. at the University of Toronto in 1953.

He began his teaching career at Senior School of Forest Lake, Minnesota, where he taught two years before entering military service. He began his college teaching at Loyola University of Los Angeles in 1954. In 1956 he joined the Marquette faculty as Assistant Professor and rose to Associate Professor in 1963 and Professor in 1968.

Professor Robb is an elected member of the Medieval Academy of America, and since 1958 has been editor of the scholarly series, Medieval Texts in Translation. In 1957 he lectured and conducted a seminar at the International Conference of Christians and Moslems (Toumliline, Morocco). His research on St. Thomas' teaching on man resulted in the first critical edition of Thomas' *Quaestiones de Anima*. In 1968 he received the Faculty Award for Teaching Excellence.

Professor Robb's publications include: "L'Education et la perfectionment de l'homme," *Confluent Revue Marocaine*, 1957; "Intelligere Intelligentibus est Esse," *An Etienne Gilson Tribute* (Milwaukee:

Marquette University Press), 1959; "St. Bernard on Twelve Degrees of Pride" and "St. Bernard on the Necessity of Loving," *Masterpieces of Catholic Literature* (Boston: Ginn), 1965; *St. Thomas Aquinas' Quaestiones de Anima* (Pontifical Institute of Medieval Studies), 1968; and articles in many journals.

To these publications Phi Sigma Tau is pleased to add: *Man as Infinite Spirit.*

Man as Infinite Spirit

"Signatum est super nos lumen vultus tui, Domine."   Ps. IV, 7.

I

In the universities of thirteenth century Europe, especially during the third quarter of the century, no topic was more widely nor more vigorously debated than the nature of man. Controversies on the nature of man, on the nature of the human soul, on the meaning and existence of intellect and of intellectual understanding raged across Europe, engaging masters from Scotland in the north to Sicily in the south. As you well know, this was the period when either new or more adequate Latin translations of the works of Aristotle and his commentators were becoming widely available. These highly sophisticated philosophical treatises, Greek, Syriac, Jewish and Arabic, forced western Christian scholars both to reformulate questions on man as an intellectual being and also to try to develop new solutions to the questions raised.

St. Thomas Aquinas, from the beginning to the end of his professional career,
never ceased to be preoccupied with questions on man, and his treatment of these
questions always presupposed a keen
awareness of what his contemporaries were
saying, and a deeply held conviction that it
was part of his responsibility as a seeker of
Christian wisdom to propose answers to
the questions being raised in his day.

Now if there is any axiom that contemporary research on St. Thomas has dis-
credited, once and for all, it is the statement
that *"Divus Thomas semper formalissime
loquitur,"* that St. Thomas always speaks
with extraordinary formal and logical precision. We shall see that at least when he
speaks about man, he is less concerned
with formal precision than with existential
fullness and depth. As I intend to make
clear in this lecture, St. Thomas was pro-
posing in the language of Aristotle,[1] and
ostensibly as an interpretation of Aristotle,
a view on man that none of the Aristotelian
commentators prior to St. Thomas' time
had ever found in Aristotle, possibly be-

cause it is not there. And this same Thomas Aquinas, great teacher as he was reputed to be, was not at all successful in conveying adequately the full originality of his own position to either his contemporaries or his later disciples. It has taken us 700 years to begin to do justice to the profound uniqueness of his doctrine on man.[2]

For the larger part of that 700 years, St. Thomas' doctrine on man was viewed as basically an Aristotelian position. Man was a rational animal, composed of soul and body, the soul playing the role of form and the body being the material element. The chief difference between St. Thomas' teaching and that of Aristotle, apart from the fact that St. Thomas' man is a creature of God, was that it seems to be clear that for St. Thomas the soul of man exists through itself, of its own right, and is therefore immortal; whereas it is not quite so certain that Aristotle taught the immortality of the human soul; this means, of course, that it is not absolutely certain that Aristotle did not hold this. Through the work of such contemporary students of St. Thomas

as the late Jacques Maritain, as Etienne
Gilson, Anton C. Pegis, and Father Gerard
Smith, S.J., we have become aware of new
perspectives on man in the doctrine of St.
Thomas Aquinas. Man is now seen in an
intensified existential dimension. We have
come to accept that St. Thomas views man
as an incarnate spirit, as diminished spirit,
as finite spirit. For a long time I accepted
all of these ways of naming man as being
consonant with my understanding of St.
Thomas, but not too long ago after pro-
longed re-reading of his texts, I suddenly
realized one fine day that I could no longer
accept the third of these three ways of
speaking. I came to the conviction that
there seems to be even something contra-
dictory in speaking about spirit as finite.
It is not easy to admit that one has long
misunderstood a thinker who has been extremely influential in one's intellectual life.
As John MacMurry says, there is a terrible
inertia in ideas;[3] once we have made up
our minds, and especially if we have held
the ideas for a long time, it is extremely
difficult for us to overcome this intellectual

inertia and to abandon our position, to admit our error, at least of perspective, and to make a new beginning. I am as guilty of this failing as anyone, but in one instance at least I strove to overcome the inertia and today's lecture is the result.

Since we have only a short time in which to treat an extremely complex topic, it is important to situate, as quickly as possible, our question in both a general and a personal perspective. The solution to the question as to whether man is finite or infinite spirit, or both, is proposed by St. Thomas within his discussions of human intellectuality and of the nature of the human intellect. And it was my discovery of certain neglected texts on the nature of the agent intellect that first alerted me to the fact that all was not well in my understanding of St. Thomas.

II. The Agent Intellect

During those thirteenth century intellectual debates to which I referred earlier, no topic engendered more controversy than the Aristotelian doctrine of the agent and possible intellects. Philosophers today are apt to bridle at the very mention of those venerable terms, but if we are willing to admit two propositions that St. Thomas was willing to admit, namely, (1) that we pass from being able to understand something to actually understanding it, and (2) that we possess the causal power to bring about this act of knowing, then we are admitting those two features of human understanding that the agent and possible intellects were proposed to explain.

I am not *directly* concerned here with one aspect of the debate, namely whether the agent and possible intellects are powers of the human soul, residing within man, or whether they are separate substances, powerful spiritual realities, existing independently and separate from human persons, and yet somehow playing a decisive role in human intellectual knowledge.

Let us admit, with an historical *dato non concesso*, that St. Thomas has vanquished the Latin Averroists of his day and established the presence within man of

these two intellectual powers. We must
certainly admit that his texts give evidence
that he thought that he had done so.[4]
Nevertheless I have discovered texts which
suggest that St. Thomas' acceptance of the
agent and possible intellects as powers
within man caused him certain difficulties.
These difficulties do not seem to have
bothered his disciples. When Thomists,
early or late, discuss this topic, and especially when they treat the human agent
intellect, they do so nearly always in either
of two contexts: (1) to establish the anti-
Averroistic position of St. Thomas, or (2)
to treat the agent intellect as a sort of *deus
ex machina,* trotted in to explain the trans-
ition in our knowledge from an experience
in the area of sensation to the abstract and
immaterial grasp of a notion that is universal and intelligible. They remain quite un-
expectedly aloof from what ought to be, or
at least so it seems to me, a primary pre-
occupation, namely, the ontological location of the agent intellect, or to put it more
simply: What does St. Thomas mean by
agent intellect and what is its existential

status? My feeling is, and I shall not try to justify it by citing texts, that St. Thomas' commentators, if they advert to the point at all, are as embarassed in trying to find a location in reality for the agent intellect as Platonists are in trying to find a local habitation for Plato's ideas. I cannot completely afford the luxury of avoiding this issue, for I think its solution is central to my understanding of St. Thomas' doctrine of man as infinite spirit.

One of St. Thomas' earliest texts poses the issue bluntly and clearly. In his *Commentary on the Sentences of Peter Lombard,* his first major work, St. Thomas, in treating the question as to whether the intellect is one and separate, rather than being one in each man, makes the following comment: "Therefore, since to receive understood species, which appertains to the possible intellect, and to make these species actually intelligible, which is the role of the agent intellect, cannot be identified, since to receive belongs to something in so far as it is potential, and to make belongs to something in so far as it is actual, it follows that it is impossible that the agent intellect and the possible intellect not be diverse powers."[5]

An objection might immediately be raised as to how principles so radically diverse and different can belong to a single substance, the human intellectual soul, which being simple, according to St. Thomas, has no parts. St. Thomas, as he does so frequently, anticipates this objection, just as Plato so often anticipated the objections of Aristotle, for he continues: "But how these two powers are rooted in a single substance is difficult to understand. For it does not seem that it could be characteristic of a single substance to be in potency with respect to all intelligible forms, as the possible intellect is, and also to be in act with respect to all such forms, as the agent intellect is, for otherwise the agent intellect could not produce all intelligible forms, since nothing acts except in so far as it is in act."[6]

As usual, St. Thomas says what he has to say with so little of a rhetorical flourish, that we are apt to miss part of what he is

saying. If through our possible intellect we
are able to know whatever is intelligible,
and in the philosophy of St. Thomas there
are no limits ultimately to what is intelligible other than the limits of being, and
being for St. Thomas comprises both the
finite and the infinite, then it is likewise
true that we possess a power of operation,
which is truly our own, rooted in each of
us, which is as fully actual as the possible
intellect is potential. That is to say, it is
actually, somehow, the likeness of all that
is or can be.

Nor can we argue that in this text the
young Frater Thomas was speaking care-
lessly or imprecisely. He makes the same
point in an even clearer and more decisive
way in his *Summa Theologiae*.[7] He is asking the same question, namely, whether
the agent intellect is grounded in our soul.
An objection has been made that if both
possible and agent intellects belong to our
soul, we should be able to understand
whatever we wish, at will, and this seems
to be against the fact. Neither the objection nor St. Thomas' full answer as such

interests me here, but rather one of the statements he makes in his reply. He says: "If the relation of the agent intellect to the possible intellect were that of a causing object to a power, as the actually visible is in relation to our power of seeing, it would follow that we would instantly understand everything, since the agent intellect is that which makes all things actual."

In speaking of the agent intellect, of the need to posit it, of its location within man, St. Thomas has said again and again that there must be a power in us, capable of making whatever is not actually intelligible to us to become intelligible to us, and since something can cause only in so far as it possesses actuality, such a power must *be in act* all that is intelligible in the universe in which we live. There is, therefore, in us, according to St. Thomas, a principle of being that is the likeness, actually and virtually, although not determinately, of all that is or can be known by us. Nor dare we forget that 'virtually' is not a weak term; after all, according to St. Thomas, God is virtually, although not formally and dis-

tinctly, the likeness of all that is or can be.[8]
Might not this similarity between our agent
intellect and God, as well as the fact that
our agent intellect has no cause of its causing—in its own order, it is simply first, and
therefore in one sense at least is an un-
caused cause—might not these character-
istics, as well as others we could point to,
be the reason why St. Thomas does not
hesitate in his *Commentary on St. Paul's
Epistle to the Romans* to call the human
soul divine, when in speaking of the work
of divine providence, he states that God
did certain things *"propter divinitatem
animae rationalis,"* "on account of the
divinity of the rational soul,"[9] or when he
speaks of that *"quod est divinum in ho-
mine,"* "that which is divine in man,"
namely, his intellectuality.[10]

There are many other important questions centering on the full meaning of
agent intellect in St. Thomas' doctrine that
await the work of serious students. This is
an area in Thomistic studies that is practi-
cally virgin territory. These studies await
other occasions, but it was the presence in

man of this extraordinary power, plenary
in actuality and causality, that made me
wonder whether we had done full justice
to the thought of St. Thomas in describing
man in his doctrine as a *finite* spirit. The
reflections which grew out of this wonder
shall be organized in the remainder of this
lecture under three main headings: first,
spirit as spirit; second, man as finite spirit;
and third, man as infinite spirit.

III. Spirit as Spirit

In his life-long, constantly renewed ef-
forts to understand man more adequately,
St. Thomas treated the question of what
man is in many texts which are usually
ignored by philosophers. Medieval thinkers, fresh from their reading of Aristotle,
Avicenna and Averroes, had no scruples as
to thinking about or speaking about angels,
whom they identified with the separate
substances of Aristotle. Philosophers today, not to mention theologians, are likely
to skip those sections of St. Thomas' works
where he treats of angels. This is unfortu-
ate, for one cannot understand St. Thomas'

teachings on man, unless he reads, not only the so-called "treatise on man" in the *Summa,* but also Thomas' texts on God and on the angels. It is a noble family to which man belongs, the glorious company of all intellectual beings.

To put the matter simply, St. Thomas, both in trying to understand the sort of a being that man is, and in trying to convey to his audience what he has discovered about the meaning of man, does so by locating man within the hierarchy of spiritual beings. Consequently, if we wish to do justice to his two-sided doctrine of man as both finite and infinite spirit, we must follow in his steps.

According to St. Thomas there are certain things that are simply true of any spiritual being, whether it be God, angels, or men. Let us set these down in summary fashion:

1) Every spiritual being, every intellectual being, is immaterial, free from the restricting and particularizing causality of matter.[11]

2) If this is so, then according to

varying degrees of immateriality will correspond varying modes of knowing.[12]

3) By the very fact of being immaterial, a being is intelligible, and for St. Thomas this means that in its very being it is in a way all being. In short, both the degrees of knowing and of knowability will correspond to modes of separation from matter.[13]

4) Intelligible being, which is the object of any intellect, is infinite, and the infinite is not simply the sum of finite elements.[14]

There is another cardinal point in St. Thomas' doctrine of knowledge that I beg leave to remind you of, namely, that all knowledge is through likeness, that the knower either is the thing known or else possesses the likeness of the known. From this follow two more points relevant to my purpose:

1) An intellect can know its object adequately, that is, know intelligible being, only if it possesses in itself the likeness of all being and of all the differences and species of being.[15]

2) Such a likeness of all being can be nothing other than an infinite nature, a universal principle of all being and of the power productive of all being—such a nature belongs to God alone.[16]

Note very carefully what St. Thomas is doing and also what he is not doing. When he establishes his hierarchy of intellectual beings, God, angels, men, he always does so in the context of their knowing all being. This he never questions. The only points at issue are the mode and means through which these intellectual beings know intelligible being, all that is or can be. Note, too, that his usual approach is from a special viewpoint, the viewpoint of likeness. From this perspective St. Thomas states that only God by His very nature or essence contains in Himself and is the universal likeness of all being. No other intellectual nature, since each is restricted to some genus and species, can itself be the universal likeness of all being. We must not forget for a moment the context. St. Thomas is speaking of both the divine nature and the created natures, not from the point of view of their being a source of the activity of knowing, but rather from the point of view of their being the *medium* of knowing, of their being a likeness through which beings are known. If creaturely intellectual natures are limited to some particular species, this does not mean that all of being is not their end; it simply means that such intellectual creatures need additional likenesses, over and above their own natures, to attain universally all being.

St. Thomas, and history shows he had reason, seemed to fear that his point would be missed. For after making the qualification of which I just spoke, he repeats: "Now from the very fact that a substance is intellectual, all being lies within the scope of its understanding."[17]

He then goes on to show how in intellectual beings, other than God, there are degrees of intellectuality corresponding to the types and number of likenesses which are required if the intellectual being is to attain its end of knowing intelligible being.

Another way to make the same point is

to say that St. Thomas is here indicating that although there is one and only one end for any intellectual being, there are many gradations of intellect, there are degrees of intellectuality, and since, as we have seen, intellectuality corresponds to immateriality, there are degrees of immateriality.

This doctrine has serious implications for St. Thomas' view of man. How is man to achieve an adequacy of likeness? Only through his compositeness, says St. Thomas, will man be an adequate knower, namely, able to know the truth, not just of knowledge, but of things. For this kind of adequate knowledge the agent and possible intellects are not enough. Why not? For at least two reasons. The possible intellect, being immaterial, can receive only universal forms, and since these forms are abstracted from the conditions of matter, they are not of themselves the proper likenesses of individual things. What is needed is a turning of intellect back to our sense representations, and in this act of reflexion (as St. Thomas calls it) man's intellect is completed and man achieves a proper likeness of things. In short, adequate human thinking or knowing is a composite activity, as man is composite. I might express this by saying that according to St. Thomas although we do not think with our imagination, we think in our imagination. The second reason has to do with the agent intellect. Although the agent intellect is the likeness of all things *virtually, eminently,* I might even say, it needs help in achieving *determinate* likenesses of things. I must try to be very precise at this point. Things do not specify our intellect. When we understand things, these things are not added to our intellect, but only their likenesses, and the production of these intelligible likenesses is the work of intellect. Within the human intellect there is nothing but the intellect. When the agent intellect disengages intelligible meaning within the sensibly given, and therewith produces an act of understanding, what is being added to the intellect are its own acts. It is merely the specification of these acts that come from things;

things explain partially why my acts of understanding are the kinds of acts they are, an act of understanding man instead of dog, for example. From this point of view it is possible to verify as strongly as from any St. Thomas' unalterable commitment to man as incarnate spirit. Neither by his intellect alone nor by sense alone is man an adequate knower. Man, through his intellect and sense powers, achieves an adequate likeness of things as given concretely in experience, and through these multi-faceted adequate likenesses knows things. This, of course, is to yield nothing to finiteness of spirit. This is rather to say that man in his very incarnateness, that is, in his finiteness, is totally a spiritual being, since he is quickened by a spiritual act of existing and finds his fulfillment and his goal only in that to which all spiritual beings aspire, the infinite in being, truth, goodness and beauty.

IV.   Spirit as Finite

Let me next locate the question of spirit as finite in a general perspective. In an age of increasing pressures toward the impersonal and the standardized, many of us have come to admire, if not always to emulate, some of those rare individuals who claim to be marching to a different drummer than that heard by the masses of men. In the area of scholarship and creative philosophic thought, however, we need to be careful. There is no virtue in being different merely for the sake of being different. Our contemporaries, eminent scholars many of them, who speak of St. Thomas' man as finite spirit, can do so with the assurance that there is no scarcity of clear texts to support their position. A person, therefore, would seem to be a little rash, or worse yet, more concerned to seek novelty than truth, if he were to try to maintain, without denying the authenticity of these clear texts just referred to, that man's finiteness is but one aspect of man's being, and that at the luminous center of St. Thomas' doctrine on man is the basic insight that man is infinite spirit, that in fact, the notion of finite spirit, taken without crucial qualifications, is a contradic-

tion in terms, and that if man is rather
both finite and infinite spirit, his infinity
comes both first and last, and man's finiteness is a way to his infinity. Yet this is what
I propose to maintain.

Let me situate the question in a more
personal perspective. For more than thirty
years, I have read and re-read St. Thomas
in an effort to grasp his doctrine more
deeply, and with his help to deepen my
own understanding of man as incarnate
spirit, and I must admit that I have never
asked his help in vain. For most of that
time I focussed on the incarnateness of
man's spirit, the deep involvement of the
human spirit in the world of matter, from
which has emerged man as historical being,
from which has issued all of our culture
and civilization, our science and technol-
ogy, our art, literature and worship. I did
this because it seemed to me that the spiritual side of man, for a variety of historical
and doctrinal reasons, had been unduly
emphasized. One time as I reread his texts
to deepen my own thinking on the meaning of spirit, it suddenly occured to me

that if matter in St. Thomas means closed-
ness, then spirit bespeaks openness. Openness to what, and to what degree, if there
be degrees to the spiritual? Are those horizons of time and eternity, of spirit and
matter, on which St. Thomas situated man,
limited horizons or are they illimitable?[18]
The very use of the word eternity suggests
the unlimited. Here the temptation can be
great; to opt for man as simply and purely
infinite spirit. But in the phrase just cited,
the word 'time' is there as well as the word
'eternity'; it was not simply spirit but incarnate spirit that I was trying to understand, and one of the first lessons I learned
as a metaphysician was that an explanation
which explains away the facts you are
trying to understand is apt to be a poor
explanation.

It is hardly necessary, in fact, to go to
the texts of St. Thomas to discover the
finitude of man. All of us can verify this in
ourselves. We began to exist; we are subject to all sorts of physical and mental limitations; we get sick, tired, lame; we have
emotional breakdowns. Even on the more

purely intellectual level nothing is more
obvious than our limited and pedestrian
ways of getting at truth, our proneness to
error, the hard work required for making
any intellectual progress, the process of
aging with the diminution of our powers,
and finally in death, we encounter the ap-
parent loss of all. St. Thomas was as much
aware of all these facts as we are since
human life was as difficult and as precari-
ous in the thirteenth century as it is today.
His preoccupation with these facts of
human experience is reflected in literally
dozens of clear texts, ready to rise up and
call anyone who would deny that St.
Thomas taught the finitude of man either
a fool or a liar.

There are in fact a number of reasons
for his stressing man's finiteness. Again
and again St. Thomas equates being a
creature with being finite.[19] Sometimes he
reverses the statement and declares that
whatever is finite is a creature.[20] From the
beginning to the end of his career, St.
Thomas distinguishes between God and
creature as between the infinite and the

finite. Obviously many reasons could be adduced, but in my view there are three basic reasons why St. Thomas calls man 'finite spirit,' but as we shall see these reasons do not prove so much as is often supposed. The first reason has to do with existence, the second with operation, the third with the distinction between our present life and the life beyond this life.

First of all, man, like any creature, is finite in the sense that he is caused to be, through secondary causes to be sure, but ultimately by the source of all existence, a loving and creative God. Existential act, which of itself bespeaks no limitation (how could it, since it is verified unconditionally in God) is limited in each creature by the essence or substance in which it is received, and doubly restricted if the subject of existence includes, as one of its essential elements, matter. There can be, for St. Thomas, only one being which is pure subsistent existence; only this being is unqualifiedly infinite.[21] Everything else, in its very act of being diverse from the First Being, falls short of this infinity and is consequently finite. Causal dependence is clearly expressed by the finiteness of creatures.[22]

The second reason, on the level of operation, becomes very obvious as soon as one extensively examines the contexts in which the term 'finite' is used most frequently. It is when St. Thomas treats of the incomprehensibility of God that he most clearly speaks of the finiteness of our intellect, of any created intellect in fact. St. Thomas uses the word 'comprehend,' just as we do, with several meanings. Sometimes although not too frequently, he means simply 'to understand,' 'to reach through one's power of understanding.' More commonly, however, St. Thomas uses the word in a high technical medieval sense, namely to indicate that whatever is comprehended is known perfectly, and that something is perfectly known only when it is known to the full and total extent of its knowability, so that nothing more could possibly remain to be known.[23] Obviously an actually infinite being cannot be known infinitely except by a knower whose power of knowing is infinite, and whose means and mode and medium of knowing are also infinite. Only God is such a being; but to say that we cannot know God comprehensively is not in the least to deny the universal openness of our intellects to the infinity of being; it is simply one of St. Thomas' ways of saying that we are not God.[24]

There is a third and extremely important reason why St. Thomas stresses finiteness. Both in his metaphysics and consequently in his philosophy of man, St. Thomas utilizes the Aristotelian doctrine of proportioned end, although it is true that he uses it in ways that Aristotle had not thought of doing. Now the proportioned end of a being can be viewed as that end which can be reached or achieved by the activities and operations which flow from that being's nature, i.e., an acorn grows into an oak, reproducing itself by producing other acorns; I, using my insight and powers of reason, develop a political philosophy or plan and raise a garden. In fact, if we do not keep in mind St. Thomas' emphasis on this notion of proportioned end, how could we possibly accept what he says about man's intellect's apprehending being, not merely as given in the present, as verified in some being which we experience here and now, but rather *being without qualification,* and at the same time accept such statements as the following: The nature of our intellect is to know species abstracted from the phantasm; for example, from my sense experience of Tom, I disengage and grasp the intellectual notion 'man.' If we read carefully, we shall notice that St. Thomas usually qualifies such statements by expressions like 'in this life.' At other times he contrasts natural knowledge and knowledge through grace.[25]

V. Spirit as Infinite

As we have just seen, there are a number of excellent reasons why St. Thomas insists that there are times when it is correct to call the human, intellectual soul, even man himself, a finite spirit. Still, he is no less emphatic in declaring that even this lowest of all intellectual substances, so far removed from the perfect and infinite intellectuality of God that St. Thomas does not hesitate to call this soul a *rusticus*,[26] a humble countryman, a simple peasant, living on the fringes of the civilized world as it were, even this diminished and impoverished intellectual substance is infinite.

The first reaction of most students of St. Thomas to that statement I have found to be either outright rejection or, at best, polite scepticism. This I can understand; we bring to each of our readings of the great philosophers both certain preconceptions and also a specific set of questions, which at that particular reading are the questions that interest us, and consequently we get answers to those question, if we get any answers at all, and our minds, open as they may be, tend to ignore anything which is not pertinent to our questions. It is hard to let our philosophical masters calmly raise their own questions and answer them in the way that suits them. One thing we can do with any thinker of the calibre of St. Thomas is to continue to return to his texts as we become aware of new questions, filled with the assurance that he will always have something more to say to us.

When I reread St. Thomas this past year
in an effort to see whether there were clear
texts to support my conviction that St.
Thomas viewed man as infinite spirit, I
discovered infinity everywhere. For example, St. Thomas raises a good medieval
question, namely, whether our intellect
can know infinite things. As ususal in a
medieval author the question is precise
and concrete. He is not asking whether
our intellect is open to the infinite, or
whether our intellect itself is infinite. The
question is whether we can know an infinite number of things. His answer to that
question is "No."[27]

In clarifying his position, he has to deal
with the following objection. Our intellect,
since it is not a power of corporeal matter,
would seem to be infinite in power. But an
infinite power can extend to an infinite
number of things. Therefore, our intellect
can know an infinite number of things.
Since this is an objection which attacks the
position he has adopted, one would expect
St. Thomas to reject it, and he does. What

is curious, however, is the way he deals
with the point raised. He writes with perfect equanimity, "In the way in which our
intellect is infinite in power, in that way
does it know the infinite. Its power is infinite because it is not terminated by corporeal matter. Furthermore our intellect
can know the universal which is abstracted
from individual matter and consequently
is not restricted to an individual, but con-
sidered in itself, the universal extends to
an infinite number of individuals."

What is St. Thomas doing? Is this some
sort of metaphysical juggling, is this a medieval metaphysical version of the Indian
rope trick where we think we see something that is not there at all? I think not;
St. Thomas is one of the most honest of
thinkers, and it is a mark of great and
honest thinkers that they never play with
ideas; they take them seriously. We can
understand better, I believe, why he can
say both of these things, that we are finite
and infinite, if we start where he first
raises the question in his *Summa Theologiae*, in the section dealing with the infin-

ity of God and of God's knowledge.[28] As a
gauge that we are not undertaking a fruit-
less quest, we have St. Thomas' assurance,
expressed in numerous texts, that nothing
prevents something from being infinite in
one mode of being, which, in another way,
is finite;[29] and we have those oft repeated,
and oft ignored, assurances that our intellect, *quoddamodo*, in some fashion, possesses infinity.

In treating the question of the infinity
of God, St. Thomas contrasts the infinity
that belongs to matter with that of form.
Infinity, as he uses the term here, means
not-finited, not terminated, limited, restricted in some fashion. Prime matter, the
ultimate undetermined stuff of the universe, acquires perfection in being united
to and structured by form. Apart from such
structuring determination, prime matter is
purely indefinite and could not exist. This
being so, material infinity means *imper-
fection*, and in being finited and deter-
mined, *matter* acquires reality and perfection. The exact opposite is true of form.
Form is open to be the form of endlessly

proliferating beings and, as such, form possesses infinity; it is through its union with matter that form is restricted to being the form of this one particular being. The termination of form by matter, therefore, has about it the notion of the imperfect; form's perfection is restricted by such termination. No one man, in short, possesses the fullness of what *man* can be. Form itself, as not terminated by matter, therefore, has about it the quality of the perfect. St. Thomas immediately meets an objector who insists that if this is so, then every intellectual created substance, since it grasps universals which can extend to an infinite number of singulars, is infinite.[30] Not so fast, rejoins St. Thomas; only God is infinite without any qualifications whatsoever, for only He is pure subsistent Spirit, and consequently the being which God is is not received in any principle, of any sort, that might contract or limit it.

St. Thomas, however, is willing to concede a crucial point to the objector. Forms received in matter, he says, are without qualification finite, and in no way infinite.

However, if there are forms, which are not received in matter, but which are subsisting forms, such as angels and human souls, then these will be in a qualified sense infinite. I realize that the translation of St. Thomas' key terms, *'simpliciter'* and *'secundum quid'* presents difficulties. A colleague of mine used to say, though not for publication, that when St. Thomas says *'simpliciter,'* he means that something is so; and when he says *'secundum quid,'* he means that something is not so. In our example, when St. Thomas declares that a created spiritual substance is infinite, *secundum quid,* he really means that it is not infinite. This will not do, however. Qualifications, even though they be but qualifications, are important, and the qualifications to which St. Thomas refers in this text are precisely those factors in being that constitute a created spiritual substance.

St. Thomas' answer to this objection is once again unusual. He does not, as one might expect him to, after concluding in the main part of the article that every being short of God is finite, reject the ob-

jector's conclusion that every created intellectual substance is infinite. Rather, he
explains, in what sense the objector's conclusion is correct, namely, because such
intellective forms are not of themselves
terminated in matter.

It would seem that in denying our intellect the power to know an infinite number of things, St. Thomas has irreparably
compromised its infinity. Not so, for in the
context in which he was writing, knowing
infinite things, one after another, is something which even God, pure infinite being,
cannot do. He clarifies the infinity of man's
spirit and at the same time points out how
our infinity falls short of the divine infinity
when he treats the question as to whether
those who see God in His very essence
comprehend Him. As we said earlier, to
comprehend something means to know
something according to the fullness of its
knowability. In this sense no creature, finite in existence, can truly comprehend God.
Only God knows God in this way. But any
intellect, seeing God is His very essence,
sees that God is infinite and infinitely know-

able, since the intellect grasps God's infinite being. However, according to the
mode through which the created intellect
knows this infinite God, the creature cannot
be said to know Him infinitely, that is, we
can know the infinite but not know it infinitely.[31]

One of the most beautiful as well as
one of the most profound texts in which
St. Thomas treats infinity of knowing is
one dealing with the question as to whether God has knowledge.[32] Knowers, St.
Thomas begins, are distinguished from beings that do not know on the grounds that
non-knowers possess only their own forms;
through its formal structure a cabbage is
simply a cabbage, and it will never be anything more so long as it remains itself.
Knowers, however, not only possess the
form by which they are themselves; they
also possess the forms of all the things they
know. This is what St. Thomas calls a
remedy that God provided for overcoming
the imperfections of individual knowers.
Each of these individual beings, consid-
ered just in itself, is only a tiny part of the

perfection of the universe, which consists
in the sum total of the perfections of all
beings.

Through knowledge the perfection that
belongs by nature to one thing is found in
another, the knower. Hence an intellectual
knower is in some fashion all things. In this
way, too, it is possible for the perfection of
the entire universe to exist in one thing. To
admit this is to admit that for knowers there
is a genuine communication in the total
perfection of the universe. The philosophers of old call this state the end of man,
namely, that in the soul might be deline-
ated the entire order and the cause of the
universe. The Christian philosopher puts
the same matter a bit differently, stating
that the end of man is the vision of God;
this of course means he knows all the universe, too, for St. Thomas quotes St. Greg-
ory, "What is there that they do not see
who see Him who sees all things?" Consequently the being of non-knowers is con-
tracted and limited, whereas the being of
knowers has a greater amplitude and ex-
tension. Now, as we have seen, the contrac-

tion of form comes through matter. Hence
the more immaterial a form is, the more
such a form approaches more nearly to
infinity.

Here we reach in a sense the central
issue. Among those beings which possess
knowledge there are degrees of immateriality, freedom from the constraining re-
striction of what is material. Immateriality,
which is present even in some degree on
the level of sensation, can be called spir-
ituality and applies in the strict sense to
those subsisting forms which can exist
apart from bodies, God, angels, and human
souls. Here, too, we have degrees of immateriality, and corresponding to these,
degrees of intellectuality, and now as well,
degrees of infinity. It came as a metaphysical shock to me many years ago when I
first learned that some spiritual substances
were more immaterial than others; not in
the sense of being less material, for no
intellectual substances contain matter, but
as being more richly and purely intellectual. Now I have had to get used to another
metaphysical shock; I am forced to admit

that in St. Thomas' doctrine infinity, like immateriality, has degrees.[33]

There are even stronger expressions that St. Thomas uses to indicate the infinity of spirit. In speaking of the operations of knowing, St. Thomas declares that the act of sensation is relatively infinite because sensation is related to all sensible things just as sight is related to all visible things, and such objects are at least potentially infinite. But, he continues, an act of understanding or an act of the will possesses infinity absolutely. Why? Because their objects are the true and the good, both of which are convertible with being, and consequently to understand and to will bear relation to all things, and each such operation is specified by its object.[34] This is in line with his so frequently cited principle that the object of the intellect is universal being or universal truth.[35]

He makes this same point in many ways, but few, if any, expressions of it are more satisfying than the following text in which St .Thomas asserts our participation in the fullness of that knowledge which is God's.

"In God," he writes, "the whole plenitude of intellectual knowledge is contained in one thing, that is to say, in the divine essence by which God knows all things. This plenitude is found in created intellects in a lower manner and less simply. Consequently it is necessary for lower intellects to know by many forms what God knows by one, and by so many the more according as the intellect is lower."[36] The important point to recall from this text is that intellectual *plenitude,* although achieved in diverse ways, is the mark of any intellect.

So strongly is St. Thomas committed to this view that he bases one of his arguments for God's infinity upon the fact that our intellect extends to the infinite in the order of understanding, and consequently there must be an infinite intelligible reality in existence, otherwise such an intellectual ordination would be in vain.[37]

The same point can be drawn from St. Thomas' doctrine of the relation between the potential and the actual; in brief, unless we are to empty the potential of all meaning, then to every potency must correspond that which would actualize it. To say that we have the potentiality to be nourished would be meaningless if there were not or could not be food. His argument here is that our intellect is in potency to all intelligible being, to all intelligible species, and such species are infinite since the species of both number and figure are infinite. Hence there must be in us a power to actualize the knowledge of such infinites and this power is, in that sense at least, infinite.[38]

This is not to say, as we have already pointed out, that our intellect knows the infinite in the way in which God knows it. The basic reason, of which we should never lose sight, is that our intellect is not infinite without qualification; its infinity is a qualified one, but in order for an infinity to be qualified, I take it that it must first be in some fashion infinite.[39]

It seems to me, therefore, if we are to understand what St. Thomas means by that paradoxical being, infinite created spirit, we must see precisely how finitude is inserted into infinity. Man, like any intellec-

tual being, is open unreservedly to the
infinity of being, truth and goodness. If
God is to share His life in friendship, then
only spiritual beings will serve. Their com-
ing into existence is a call, a vocation, ad-
dressed to them by God to share His life
and light and thereby attain beatitude. But
along with this created openness to the
infinite comes creaturely causality, including man's freedom. A true Christian humanism has nothing to fear from man's
relation to God. Since it is the relation that
bestows on man his proper infinity, how
could we ever view this relationship as
enslaving!

Man's intellect, the lowest of all intellects, comes into being in a state of pure
potentiality, actually knowing nothing,
able to know all. Man's incarnateness, his
involvement with the world of matter and
change, of time and space, is both the mark
and the measure of his lowliness as spirit,
but is also the mode and means of his fulfillment. Working, in this life, among the
kind of intelligibility that is itself 'incarnate,' i.e., embodied, found in material

substances, man nevertheless grasps more than these beings; he attains being.[40] And it is with this same intellect that man may some day see God. Through the finite to the infinite, for the intelligibility we disengage is still creaturely and therefore in some sense finite; and even the light of glory which will enable us to withstand our seeing God, though it be a grace, is still a creature. None of this would be sufficient, singly or together, if the intellect itself did not mean infinite. As Soame Jenyns declares, God cannot instruct a mole in astronomy or an oyster in music. When we examine man here and now, it is as if we have broken in on a conversation already in progress. Each word bespeaks finitude. But the first word and the last word is infinity, and infinity subtends and ultimately supports and crowns every thought and deed of man.

If this be so, why does St. Thomas so frequently speak of man as finite. For the same reason that he so often speaks of man as animal; and yet we do not conclude that St. Thomas is reducing man to his animal-ity, nor is he therefore reducing the infinity of spirit to finiteness. In line with his pre-occupation, common to all the great thinkers who have reflected on and spoken about God, not to compromise in any way the unqualified infinity, the total incomprehensibility, the utter ineffability of God, St. Thomas uses a great variety of expressions to qualify in some way the grasp that created infinite spirit has on uncreated infinite spirit, but let me remind you once again, one can qualify the infinite as being finite from a certain perspective only if there be an infinite to be so qualified.

St. Thomas will say, for example, that the truth of the divine essence exceeds the light of any created intellect, and hence it is impossible that any creature see God, *ita perfecte*, as perfectly as God can be seen, and hence no created intellect can comprehend God.[41] That of course is not in question. The creature does see God, who is the infinite in being, essence and power. Or St. Thomas will say, "The saints will see the fullness of the divine essence when they reach their homeland, but not

fully," *totam essentiam . . . sed non totaliter.*[42] Or he will say, "Anything is knowable
to the degree that it is a being and is true;
but the divine being is infinite, as likewise
is its truth. Therefore God is infinitely
knowable. But no creature can know infinitely (mode) even if what it knows be
infinite. Hence no creature can comprehend God in seeing Him."[43]

Or again, "Our intellect can understand the whole God, but not wholly. With
God, one must know the whole or nothing
at all, since in Him there is no question of
part or whole. I say 'not wholly' however,
since the intellect does not know Him perfectly in so far as He is knowable by His
very nature."[44]

Another way of speaking is to speak of
something being infinite *extensively*, that
is, it extends to an infinity, and yet being
finite *intensively*. Thus we could speak of
our intellect as open to all being from the
very fact that it is immaterial, and hence
is extensively infinite; but we shall never
grasp, even in glory, the infinity of being
as unconditionally as it is knowable, and

hence our knowledge of being is intensively finite.[45]

St. Thomas also speaks of the *efficacy* of a knowing power when he discusses our seeing the essence of God. We shall see the self-same reality that God sees, he proclaims, namely, His essence, *"sed non ita efficaciter,"* but not so fully as God does.[46] Another term St. Thomas utilized in describing the fullness of knowledge to which we are ordered is the adverb *plenissime, "ad omnia plenissime cognoscenda."* We are oriented toward the amplest, most abundant, fullest knowledge of all things.[47]

In short, there can be no doubt in the mind of St. Thomas as to our openness to the fullness of being, to the infinity which both being and God are. We begin as infinite potentiality; we are ordered to infinite actualization; and our finiteness merely indicates the mode through which we make progress toward our goal. All St. Thomas ever does is to qualify to some degree our imperfections as creaturely knowers, imperfections of which we all are, alas, only too well aware. Open to the fullness of be-

ing we are; made for infinity, we are; made
to reach the plenitude which God is, un-
questionably; but we shall not attain it
intensively, comprehensively, perfectly,
nor with total clarity.[48]

VI. Conclusion

St. Thomas' purpose was not merely to
answer questions, but rather to understand
reality, in this instance, man. St. Thomas
saw man both as finite spirit and as infinite
spirit; he felt that both the finitude and the
infinity of man ought to be stressed, not
merely because they are both true, but because each attribute could serve to point a
lesson to the men of his time. Man's proper
finitude was a salutary lesson in humility
for those Latin Averroists in Paris who
seemed to think they could syllogize their
way into heaven. They denied the need for
revelation, for theology and for grace. Man
with his own unaided intellectual powers
was self-sufficient and autonomous. It was
not philosophy itself but the notion of the
total self-sufficiency of philosophy that St.

Thomas, as well as St. Bonaventure, criticized.

However, there were other men around who had another and an opposed attitude, a far less optimistic view of the range of human reason. St. Thomas was in Paris when the impetuous Bishop Etienne Tempier condemned certain philosophical propositions in 1270. Though he did not live to see it, St. Thomas was active enough in the intellectual life of Paris to anticipate the great condemnations of 1277, when some of his own doctrines were to be condemned. One of the upshots of this condemnation, launched at the philosophers or philosophizing theologians of the time, was a notable decline in human reason's assurance at being able to do its own work. The spirit of the late thirteenth and early fourteenth centuries is less audacious, less optimistic, less sure of itself than it had been in St. Thomas' day. The men of that time might have found inspiration and a charter of freedom in St. Thomas' view of man as infinite spirit.

Our own age is in as deep a need for

both of these insights as was St. Thomas'
own. We have specialists in many fields
who imperialistically claim competence to
settle all ultimate questions through their
own particular disciplines. Such people
need to be reminded of man as finite. There
are others who, having no sense of the metaphysical notion of intentionality, would
reduce human knowing to the material and
physical conditions which accompany it.
As Dr. Samuel Johnson said: The rights of
nations and of kings sink into questions of
grammar if grammarians discuss them. In
St. Thomas' language, they do not know
the difference between physical being and
intelligible being. Follow them and there
is no metaphysics of knowledge or of love,
in fact no metaphysics worthy of the name.
Perhaps they have loved darkness more
than light. Such men need a glimpse of the
vision which St. Thomas expressed in call-
ing man infinite spirit. This latter way of
describing man seems to be more true than
the first, for it includes the other. Man's
particular kind of infinity, and infinite he
is, is the sort which has marks of finitude

about it, just as man's intellectuality is an incarnate one.

If you wish to stress the dependence of man on his creative source, his creaturely status, his fallibility in knowing and loving, his imperfections and limitations, then by all means call him finite spirit. But if in these troubled times, when it is all too easy to grow pessimistic and cynical, if you wish to stress man's true fellowship with God and with all other spiritual beings; if you wish to stress man's openness to the fullness of existential reality, man as someone whose very ontological structure guarantees the possibility of metaphysics, and explains man's permanent refusal to deny the metaphysical dimensions either of himself or of the universe; if you wish to emphasize the illimitable horizons and catch a glimpse of that partnership which is possible between the Spirit which God is and the spirit which is man, a partnership in which the very meaning of God's infinite power is seen as meaning that in this world, through the difficult yet cooperative work between infinite uncreated Spirit and infinite created spirit, all things, even a new heaven and a new earth are possible, then, on this day, when we have gathered to celebrate the 700th anniversary of his death and of the day on which, I am sure, he entered into glory and into light, then, along with him, whom I gratefully call my master in Christian wisdom, St. Thomas Aquinas, name man infinite and everlasting spirit.

NOTES

1.   "Alia opinio est Aristotelis quam omnes mod-
erni sequuntur. quod anima unitur corpori sicut
forma materiae." *In III Sent.*, dist. 5, q. 3, a. 2;
ed. M. F. Moos (Paris, P. Lethielleux, 1933),
p. 207.
2.   Cf. Anton C. Pegis, "St. Thomas and the
Unity of Man," in *Progress in Philosophy.* ed.
James A. McWilliams, S.J. (Milwaukee, Bruce,
1955), pp. 153-173.
3.   John Macmurray, "The Nature and Function
of Ideologies," in Murray, J. Middleton, *et al.*,
Marxism (London, Chapman and Hall, 1935),
pp. 63-66.
4.   Pegis, *ibid.*
5.   *In II Sent.*, dist. 17, q. 2, a. 1. "Cum ergo recipere species intellectas, quod est intellectus possibilis, et facere eas intelligibiles actu, quod est
intellectus agentis, non possint secundum idem
convenire; sed recipere convenit alicui secundum quod est in potentia, et facere secundum
quod est in actu: impossibile est agentem et
possibilem non esse diversas potentias." ed. P.
Mandonnet, (Paris, P. Lethielleux, 1929), Vol.
II, p. 428.
6.   *Ibid.*, "Sed quomodo possint radicari in una
substantia est difficile videre: non enim videtur
quod uni substantiae possit convenire esse in
potentia respectu omnium formarum intelligi-
bilium, quod est intellectus possibilis, et esse
actu respectu omnium illarum, quod est intellectus agentis: alias non posset facere omnes formas
intelligibiles, cum nihil agat nisi secundum quod
est in actu."
7.   *Summa Theologiae,* I, q. 79, a. 4, obj. 3 and

ad 3. I am not including references to any edition of the *Summa Theologiae;* there are a great many editions, and besides because of the relative brevity of texts in the *Summa,* it is usually not time-consuming to find the text referred to.

8.   *Summa Theologiae,* I, q. 4, a. 2.

9.   *Expositio in V. Rom.,* lectio 3; (Turin, Marietti, 1929) Vol. I, p. 73.

10. *Expositio in I Rom.,* lectio 7; *ed. cit.,* Vol. I, p. 25.

11. Any number of texts could be cited to reinforce this point. One of St. Thomas' earliest texts is *In II Sent.,* dist. 3, q. 1, a. 1; *ed. cit.,* Vol. II, p. 86, where he insists that no intellectual being contains matter. Cf. also the following texts: *Summa Theologiae,* I. q. 14, a. 1; I, q. 79, a. 1, ad 4; I, q. 105, a. 3; *De Veritate,* q. 2, a. 2; (Rome, Leonine ed., 1970) Tome XXII, Vol. I, Fasc. 2, pp. 42-47; q. 23, a. 1 (The present Leonine published text ends with question 20.); *Compendium Theologiae,* cap. 28, 75; in *Opuscula Theologica,* ed. R. Verardo (Turin, Rome, Marietti, 1954) Vol. I, p. 21 and p. 36; *Quaestiones de Anima,* q. 13; ed. James H. Robb (Toronto, Pontifical Institute of Mediaeval Studies, 1968) pp. 185-196; *In I Sent.,* dist. 35, q. 1, a. 1, *ed. cit.,* pp. 808-813.

12. Once again there is no paucity of texts. I shall cite only texts of major importance, and not all of them. Cf. *Summa Contra Gentiles,* II, 98; editio Leonina manualis; (Turin, Rome, Marietti, 1946) pp. 220-223. The whole series of chapters 90 through 101 might profitably be read with this particular question in mind; *Summa Theologiae,* I. q. 56, a. 1; I, q. 79, a. 2; I, q. 105, a. 3; *De Veritate,* q. 2, a. 2; *ed. cit.,* pp. 42-47; q.

2, a. 5; *ed cit.*, pp. 59-65; q. 8, a.6; *ed. cit.*, pp. 236-239; q. 8, a. 9; *ed. cit.*, pp. 248-251; q. 8, a. 11; *ed. cit.*, 253-257; q. 10, a. 8; *ed. cit.*, pp. 318-326;*Quaestiones de Anima*, q. 7; *ed. cit.*, pp. 116-127; *De Substantiis Separatis*, cap. 14; *Compendium Theologiae*, cap. 30; *ed. cit.*, p. 22; and cap. 80-83; pp. 38-39.

13.   On this point see especially *Summa Contra Gentiles*, II, 98; *ed. cit.*, pp. 220-223. Cf. also *De Veritate*, q. 15, a. 2; *ed. cit.*, Vol. II, pp. 483-489.

14.   *Summa Contra Gentiles*, II, 98; *ed. cit.*, p. 221. Cf. also *Summa Theologiae*, I, q. 54, a. 2; an excellent text in I-II, q. 3, a. 7, corpus, makes the point that participated truths do not satisfy an intellect.

15.   *Summa Contra Gentiles*, II, 98.

16.   *Ibid.*

17.   *Ibid.*

18.   Cf. *Quaestiones de Anima*, q. 1, corpus. *ed. cit.* pp. 57-60.

19.   *In I Sent.*, dist. 17, q. 1, a. 1, obj. 5; *ed. cit.*, Vol. I, p. 392.

20.   *In I Sent.*, dist. 17, q. 1, a. 1, Sed contra 1; *ed. cit.*, Vol. I, p. 393.

21.   Cf. *Summa Theologiae*, I, q. 50, a. 2, ad 4.

22.   On this point read first the text in the *Summa Theologiae*, I, q. 7, a. 1 and a. 2. The same point will be made each time St. Thomas discusses the knowledge of angels and of men. For example, cf. *Summa Theologiae*, I. q. 54, a. 1, 2 and 3, and q. 75, a. 5.

23.   Sometimes, too, comprehend means simply to attain something. Cf. *Summa Theologiae*, I, q. 12, a. 7, ad 1.

24.   *Summa Theologiae*, I. q. 12, a. 7. The texts on this point are found everywhere in St.

Thomas' writings. Let me indicate only a few of the major ones: *In IV Sent.*, dist. 49, q. 2, a. 1, a. 3, a. 5, a. 6. Moos' edition of Book IV of the *Scriptum* ends with Distinction 40. For these later texts, I have used the *Opera Omina,* Tom. VII, Vol. II (Parma, 1858). The page references for the texts just cited are: pp. 1196-1201; pp. 1202-1204; pp. 1205-1207; pp. 1207-1209; Cf. also *Summa Contra Gentiles,* III, cap. 55-60; *ed. cit.,* pp. 286-292; *De Veritate,* Vol. I, q. 8, a. 2; *ed. cit.,* pp. 220-223. As I continue to read St. Thomas, I grow increasingly aware that in the vast majority of instances in which he speaks of the finiteness of created spirits, he does so in the context of what it would mean for such a spirit to *comprehend* God.

25. Cf. *Summa Theologiae,* I, q. 84, a. 7, corpus, and I, q. 87, a. 1, corpus.

26. *Summa Contra Gentiles* III, 49; *ed. cit.,* pp. 279-281.

27. *Summa Theologiae,* I. q. 86, a. 2, especially objection 4 and ad 4.

28. *Summa Theologiae,* I. q. 7, q. 12 and q. 14.

29. Cf. *In II Sent.,* dist. 17, q. 2, a. 1; *ed. cit.,* Vol. II, p. 428; *Summa Theologiae,* III, q. 10, a. 3, ad 2.

30. *Summa Theologiae,* I, q. 7, a. 2, obj. 2 and ad 2: "Quidquid habet virtutem infinitam, habet essentiam infinitam. Sed intellectus creatus habet virtutem infinitam; apprehendit enim universale, quod se potest extendere ad infinita singularia. Ergo omnis substantiae intellectualis creata est infinita. Ad secundum. Dicendum quod hoc ipsum quod virtus intellectus extendit se quodammodo ad infinita, procedit ex hoc quod intellectus est forma non in materia; sed

vel totaliter separata, sicut sunt substantiae an-
gelorum; vel ad minus potentia intellectiva, quae
non est actus alicuius organi, in anima intellectiva corpori coniuncta."

31. *Suma Theologiae,* I, q. 12, a. 7, corpus and
ad 3.

32. *De Veritate,* q. 2, a. 1; *ed. cit.,* Vol I, pp.
37-42.

33. *Summa Theologiae,* I, q. 14, a. 1.

34. *Summa Theologiae,* I, q. 54, a. 2, corpus.

35. *Summa Theologiae,* I, q. 55, a. 1, corpus.

36. *Summa Theologiae,* I, q. 55, a. 3, corpus.

37. *Summa Contra Gentiles,* I, 43: *ed. cit.,* pp.
41-43.

38. *Summa Contra Gentiles,* I, 69; *ed. cit.,* pp.
64-66, but especially p. 65.

39. *Ibid.* Here once again I could cite dozens of
texts which make the same point. Let me cite as
typical the following: *Summa Contra Gentiles,*
II, 49; *ed. cit.,* pp. 142-143; *De Veritate,* q. 15,
a. 2; *ed. cit.* Vol II, pp. 483-489; q. 18, a. 1; Vol.
II, pp. 529-535; q. 20, a. 4; Vol. II, pp. 579-585.
This last text is especially fine in clarifying St.
Thomas' usage of the terms 'finite' and 'infinite'
as applied to God and to created knowers.

40. Cf. James H. Robb, "Intelligere Intelligentibus est Esse," in *An Etienne Gilson Tribute.* ed.
Charles J. O'Neil (Milwaukee, Marquette University Press, 1959) pp. 209-227.

41. *In IV Sent.,* dist. 49, q. 2, a. 3, corpus ad
finem; *ed. cit.,* p. 1203.

42. *Ibid.,* ad 3; p. 1204.

43. *Compendium Theologiae,* cap. 216; *ed. cit.,*
pp. 102-105.

44. *De Veritate,* q. 2, a. 1, ad 3; *ed cit.,* Vol. I,
pp. 40-41.

45. *De Veritate,* q. 2, a. 9, corpus; *ed. cit.,* Vol. I, pp. 72-73; cf. also *De Veritate,* q. 20, a. 4, obj. 14; Vol. II, p. 580; also *De Veritate,* q. 2, a. 1, ad 10; Vol. I. p. 42.

46. *In IV Sent.,* dist. 49, q. 2, a. 1, ad 2; *ed. cit.,* p. 1199. How 'infinite' can refer to the efficacy of knowledge is clearly explained in *De Veritate,* q. 2, a. 2, ad 9; *ed. cit.,* Vol. I, p. 47.

47. *Quaestiones de Anima,* q. 15, corpus ad finem; *ed. cit.,* p. 214.

48. On the adverb *'perfecte,'* cf. *Expositio in 11 Rom.* lect. 5; *ed. cit.,* Vol. I, p. 166. On "seeing" God "clearly," cf. *De Veritate,* q. 2, a. 2, ad 5; *ed. cit.,* p. 46; also *In III Sent.,* dist. 14, a. 2, q. 2, ad 2; *ed. cit.,* pp. 448-449. A splendid treatment of this point is found in the *Scriptum.* Cf. *In III Sent.,* dist. 27, q. 3, a. 2, Responsio; *ed. cit.,* pp. 895-896.

The Aquinas Lectures

Published by the Marquette University Press
Milwaukee, Wisconsin 53233

Humanism and Theology (1943) by Werner Jaeger, Ph.D., Litt.D., (1888-1961) University professor, Harvard University. sbn 87462-107-0

The Nature and Origins of Scientism (1944) by John Wellmuth. sbn 87462-108-9

Cicero in the Courtroom of St. Thomas Aquinas (1945) by E. K. Rand, Ph.D., Litt.D., LL.D., (1871-1945) Pope professor of Latin, *emeritus,* Harvard University. sbn 87462-109-7

St. Thomas and Epistemology (1946) by Louis-Marie Regis, O.P., Th.L., Ph.D., director of the Albert the Great Institute of Mediaeval Studies, University of Montreal.

sbn 87462-110-0

St. Thomas and the Greek Moralists (1947, Spring) by Vernon J. Bourke, Ph.D., professor of philosophy, St. Louis University, St. Louis, Missouri. sbn 87462-111-9

History of Philosophy and Philosophical Education (1947, Fall) by Etienne Gilson of the *Académie française,* director of studies and professor of the history of Mediaeval philosophy, Pontifical Institute of Mediaeval Studies, Toronto. sbn 87462-112-7

The Natural Desire for God (1948) by William R. O'Connor, S.T.L., Ph.D., former professor of dogmatic theology, St. Joseph's Seminary, Dunwoodie, N.Y. sbn 87462-113-5

St. Thomas and the World State (1949) by Robert M. Hutchins, former Chancellor of the University of Chicago, president of the Fund for the Republic. sbn 87462-114-3

Method in Metaphysics (1950) by Robert J. Henle, S.J., Ph.D., academic vice-president, St. Louis University, St. Louis, Missouri.
sbn 87462-115-1

Wisdom and Love in St. Thomas Aquinas (1951) by Étienne Gilson of the *Académie française*, director of studies and professor of the history of Mediaeval philosophy, Pontifical Institute of Mediaeval Studies, Toronto.
sbn 87462-116-X

The Good in Existential Metaphysics (1952) by Elizabeth G. Salmon, Ph.D., professor of philosophy in the graduate school, Fordham University. sbn 87462-117-8

St. Thomas and the Object of Geometry (1953) by Vincent Edward Smith, Ph.D., director, Philosophy of Science Institute, St. John's University. sbn 87462-118-6

Realism and Nominalism Revisited (1954) by Henry Veatch, Ph.D., professor and chairman of the department of philosophy, Northwestern University. sbn 87462-119-4

Imprudence in St. Thomas Aquinas (1955) by Charles J. O'Neil, Ph.D., professor of philosophy, Villanova University. sbn 87462-120-8

The Truth That Frees (1956) by Gerard Smith, S.J., Ph.D., professor of philosophy, Marquette University.   sBN 87462-121-6

St. Thomas and the Future of Metaphysics (1957) by Joseph Owens, C.Ss.R., Ph.D., professor of philosophy, Pontifical Institute of Mediaeval Studies, Toronto.   sBN 87462-122-4

Thomas and the Physics of 1958: A Confrontation (1958) by Henry Margenau, Ph.D., Eugene Higgins professor of physics and natural philosophy, Yale University.
                                                                 sBN 87462-123-2

Metaphysics and Ideology (1959) by Wm. Oliver Martin, Ph.D., professor of philosophy, University of Rhode Island.   sBN 87462-124-0

Language, Truth and Poetry (1960) by Victor M. Hamm, Ph.D., professor of English, Marquette University.   sBN 87462-125-9

Metaphysics and Historicity (1961) by Emil L. Fackenheim, Ph.D., professor of philosophy, University of Toronto.   sBN 87462-126-7

The Lure of Wisdom (1962) by James D. Collins, Ph.D., professor of philosophy, St. Louis University.   sBN 87462-127-5

Religion and Art (1963) by Paul Weiss, Ph.D. Sterling professor of philosophy, Yale University.   sBN 87462-128-3

St. Thomas and Philosophy (1964) by Anton C. Pegis, Ph.D., professor of philosophy, Pontifical Institute of Mediaeval Studies, Toronto.

SBN 87462-129-1

The University In Process (1965) by John O. Riedl, Ph.D., dean of faculty, Queensboro Community College.

SBN 87462-130-5

The Pragmatic Meaning of God (1966) by Robert O. Johann, associate professor of philosophy, Fordham University.

SBN 87462-131-3

Religion and Empiricism (1967) by John E. Smith, Ph.D., professor of philosophy, Yale University.

SBN 87462-132-1

The Subject (1968) by Bernard Lonergan, S.J., S.T.D., professor of Dogmatic Theory, Regis College, Ontario and Gregorian University, Rome.

SBN 87462·133-X

Beyond Trinity (1969) by Bernard J. Cooke, S.T.D.

SBN 87462-134-8

Ideas and Concepts (1970) by Julius R. Weinberg, Ph.D., (1908-1971) Vilas Professor of Philosophy, University of Wisconsin.

SBN 87462-135-6

Reason and Faith Revisited (1971) by Francis H. Parker, Ph.D., head of the philosophy department, Purdue University, Lafayette, Indiana.

SBN 87462-136-4

Psyche and Cerebrum (1972) by John N. Findlay, M.A. Oxon., Ph.D., Clark Professor of Moral Philosophy and Metaphysics, Yale University.
ISBN 0-87462-137-2

The Problem of the Criterion (1973) by Roderick M. Chisholm, Ph.D., Andrew W. Mellon Professor in the Humanities, Brown University.
ISBN 0-87462-138-0

Man as Infinite Spirit (1974) by James H. Robb, Ph.D., professor of philosophy, Marquette University.
ISBN 0-87462-139-9

Uniform format, cover and binding.